GRIEVING AN ABUSER

*Journal Prompts to Process the
Death of Someone who Wasn't
Always Good to You*

A NOTE FROM THE AUTHOR

Dear Reader,

First, I am so sorry for your loss. I'm sure there are a lot of complicated and perhaps conflicting emotions going on right now.

Second, this book was created for you. This journal is designed to be a framework for you to untangle the emotional knots after experiencing a loss.

It is not meant to be a replacement for the support you may need from friends or family. Nor does it offer the same benefits that professional counseling offers. This book is not meant to give you the peace you may find from a higher power. It won't allow you to reconcile with the deceased, even if you wanted a reconciliation But this book may help when you just can't get support in those other areas, for whatever reason.

I wrote this book so that you know you are not alone. Your grief is unique, as are your specific experiences. Your story is worth exploring, even if it's not a linear story. The prompts are designed for you to reflect and crystalize some of what you are feeling. I hope you find safety in your journaling. I hope that through some of the prompts, that you begin to heal.

Grief is not something that can be neatly wrapped in a bow. By the end of this journal, you will still have your grief. But it is my hope that as you work through the following pages, your grief feels a little lighter.

With Love,
The Author

HOW TO USE THIS JOURNAL:

There is no right or wrong way to use this journal. There are 73 different prompts that ask you to answer a question, describe your feelings, or reflect on a certain thing.

There are eight different sections in this book. You will find prompts in each of the following topic areas:

Your Loss
Details
Your Feelings
Right to Grieve
Remembering
Relationships
Afterward
Letters

The relationship you had with the person who died was unique, so each prompt may not feel relevant or applicable to your story. You can choose to write on each page or leave blanks, complete them in order or jump around. This journal is designed to be used however you see fit. Some prompts will be harder to answer than others, but you are encouraged to lean into your emotions as you address the hard ones. It may not feel good in the moment, but you may be grateful to get some things off your chest as words flow from pen to paper.

THIS JOURNAL BELONGS TO:

IN ACKNOWLEDGEMENT OF THE
DEATH OF:

YOUR LOSS

Take some time to write about the person who died.

The first few prompts will help you reflect on their life and the memories you will carry of them.

DATE:

Who is this journal about? Who were they to you?

DATE:

How long did you know them? How did your
relationship start?

_____

_____

_____

_____

_____

_____

_____

_____

_____

_____

_____

_____

_____

_____

_____

_____

_____

_____

DATE:

At the time of their death, what did your relationship
with them look like?

DATE:

Was there ever a time before their death that you
had a positive relationship with them?

DATE:

Did you ever hope that your relationship with the
person would eventually get better?

DETATLS

Write about as many details of their death as you feel comfortable with. If there is a prompt that feels too hard to answer, skip it.

This journal is a safe space for you. You will write if and when you are ready. Remember, there are no right or wrong answers. Blank spaces are allowed.

DATE:

Did you feel prepared for the death of this person?
Was it a surprise?

DATE:

Was their death sudden or prolonged?

DATE:

How did they die? Feel free to include as many
details as you feel comfortable with.

DATE:

How did you first find out about their death?

DATE:

What do you remember feeling when you learned that they had died? Was it more than one feeling at once?

DATE:

Did you ever feel the need to protect them when
they were alive?

DATE:

Do you feel the need to protect them now, in death?

DATE:

Have you ever made excuses for their bad behavior?

DATE:

Is there anything you wish this person would
apologize to you about?

DATE:

Is there anything you wish you could apologize to
this person about?

DATE:

Can you forgive them? Do you want to forgive them?

DATE:

In the wake of this person's death, are there
memories that have been brought up for you that
you hadn't thought about in years?

YOUR FEELINGS

You. Your grief. No one knows exactly how you feel, but the next few pages are designed for you to help sort out your thoughts and feelings for your own purposes.

If you are not ready, you can always skip a page and come back later when it feels better. Your experiences are valid and you are allowed to feel exactly as you do.

This is your story.

DATE:

Have you found yourself returning to any old
patterns of thinking or feeling?

DATE:

Do you find yourself bouncing between emotions, or staying in a couple of stonger emotions for longer periods of time?

DATE:

Have you experienced frustration or disappointment
that life has not turned out differently?

DATE:

Is there a part of you that feels relieved now that this person is dead?

DATE:

What are your hopes and fears as you move forward?

DATE:

What gives you comfort?

DATE:

The hardest part emotionally has been:

DATE:

Are there any aspects of your life that indicate to you
that you are healing?

_____

_____

_____

_____

_____

_____

_____

_____

_____

_____

_____

_____

_____

_____

_____

_____

_____

_____

_____

_____

THE RIGHT TO GRIEVE

Take some time to write about your grief.

The first few prompts will help you reflect on your grieving process.

DATE:

Do you feel rushed to complete the grieving process
in order to get back to normal?

DATE:

How does it feel when someone expresses their
sympathy to you, not knowing the whole story?

DATE:

Do words of sympathy feel hollow to you? Painful?
Shameful?

DATE:

Do you feel supported in taking as long as you need
to process your emotions?

_____

_____

_____

_____

_____

_____

_____

_____

_____

_____

_____

_____

_____

_____

_____

_____

DATE:

Have you felt the urge to ask for help and decided
against it?

DATE:

Did you receive any well meaning but hurtful
comments from friends or family after you told
them about your loss?

_____

_____

_____

_____

_____

_____

_____

_____

_____

_____

_____

_____

_____

_____

_____

_____

_____

_____

_____

DATE:

Do you have any special objects or possessions that once belonged to your person? Why did you choose to keep that item in particular?

DATE:

Have you felt that your pain has been ignored or
overlooked by others? How has that felt?

DATE:

Do you feel like you have to put on a show for others
when you express your grief?

DATE:

Have you ever felt like someone was trying to take
your grief away from you?

DATE:

What are some avenues of support you have for dealing with your grief?

_____

_____

_____

_____

_____

_____

_____

_____

_____

_____

_____

_____

_____

_____

_____

_____

_____

DATE:

Have you had trouble concentrating on tasks and
instead find yourself thinking about your person?
How has this affected your work or family life?

DATE:

Do you feel frustrated if you cant concentrate on the things you "should" be concentrating on?

DATE:

Have you had a negative attitude or thoughts that
keep running through your head?

_____

_____

_____

_____

_____

_____

_____

_____

_____

_____

_____

_____

_____

_____

_____

_____

DATE:

Thoughts I know are not true but I can't help from thinking are:

_____

_____

_____

_____

_____

_____

_____

_____

_____

_____

_____

_____

_____

_____

_____

_____

_____

_____

DATE:

The thing I hate to admit most is:

REMEMBERING

Reflecting on the life of your person and the relationship that you had with them can be challenging, cathartic, or both at the same time.

This section will help you reflect on the memories of the person who died.

DATE:

What is something that reminds you of this person?

DATE:

Are there any habits and memories that make it seem
as if this person is still alive?

_____

_____

_____

_____

_____

_____

_____

_____

_____

_____

_____

_____

_____

_____

_____

_____

_____

_____

DATE:

Do you have any happy memories of this person?

DATE:

Is there an aspect of your relationship that you will
miss?

DATE:

What was a good quality about this person?

DATE:

Does your truth complicate the way others might
grieve the death of this person?

DATE:

Do you think your truth would cause others to
remember this person differently?

DATE:

Do you want others to know the truth so that they
will be forced to remember this person differently?

RELATIONSHIPS

The next few prompts will help you to consider the support you have gotten from your partner, friends or family, or what support has been lacking.

No matter what your close relationships look like, you may choose to respond to the prompts as you feel. You may also choose to skip them.

DATE:

Do you have a friend or family member who has
been a compassionate listener or trusted confidant
during this time?

DATE:

What are some words or actions people have said or
done that have shown their concern for you? You can
choose to list as many as possible or write down what
has felt most meaningful.

DATE:

Is this the most significant death you have
experienced? How does it differ from other deaths
you have experienced?

DATE:

Has this death affected your other close relationships?

DATE:

How has your partner or family given you support?

DATE:

How have you been able to support your partner or family?

DATE:

Is there anyone you feel like you have been able to
confide in to tell them about your conflicting
feelings?

DATE:

If you have told someone else, how far did you
share? If you havent told anyone, what would you
want them to know?

AFTERWARD

In the weeks and months that follow your loss, you have continued to keep going.

This section will help you reflect on the events after your loss and your emotions surrounding them.

DATE:

What do you need for life to make sense again?

DATE:

Because of their death, are there any other aspects of life that you also question?

DATE:

What have you been doing to heal?

DATE:

What feels discouraging when you think about creating a new future?

DATE:

What uncertainties do you have right now?

DATE:

What support have you had since this person's death?

DATE:

Where have you found small moments of joy?

DATE:

How have you been reorienting yourself? Where do you go from here?

DATE:

How have you felt healing?
What activities feel soul-soothing?

DATE:

What are some comforting words that you have found meaning in?

DATE:

What are you grateful for?

DATE:

What other resorces have felt helpful, even if only a little?

DATE:

Is there anything you want to do or accomplish in
the memory of (or in spite of) this person's life?

DATE:

How do you want others to remember them?

LETTERS

If you have made it this far in the book, you have put in significant time and energy to address your loss and your healing. Now just two prompts remain: letter writing.

The first letter is for the person who died. What message do you want to send them? What do you want them to know?

The second letter is to be written to you. So much of this journal is about the person who died, but you are still here. You are the vessel that acknowledges the past and chooses to move into the future. What do you need to say to yourself? Do you need to cut yourself some slack? Be more patient with your competing emotions? What does it mean for you to keep living?

This section will help you crystalize your feelings toward your person. It will also help you identify your inner stregth in the face of loss.

DATE:

Write a letter to your less than loved one.

DATE:

Write a letter to yourself.

Made in United States
North Haven, CT
27 February 2024

49321603R00055